DINOSAURS
AROUND THE WORLD

A⁺

Smart Apple Media

Published by Smart Apple Media, an imprint of Black Rabbit Books
P.O. Box 3263, Mankato, Minnesota 56002
www.blackrabbitbooks.com

Library of Congress Cataloging-in-Publication Data

Alderton, David, 1956- author.
 Dinosaurs around the world / contributing authors, David Alderton [and nine others] ; consulting editor, Per
Christiansen ; series editor, Sarah Uttridge.
    pages cm. -- (Animals around the world)
 Audience: Grades 4 to 6.
 Includes index.
 ISBN 978-1-62588-192-2
 1. Dinosaurs--Juvenile literature. I. Christiansen, Per, author, editor. II. Uttridge, Sarah, author, editor. III. Title.
 QE861.5.A397 2015
 567.91--dc23
                           2013045542

Contributing Authors: David Alderton, Susan Barraclough, Per Christiansen, Kieron Connolly,
Paula Hammond, Tom Jackson, Claudia Martin, Carl Mehling, Veronica Ross, Sarah Uttridge
Consulting Editor: Per Christiansen
Series Editor: Sarah Uttridge
Editorial Assistant: Kieron Connolly
Designer: Andrew Easton
Picture Research: Terry Forshaw

Printed in the United States at Corporate Graphics, Mankato, Minnesota
4-2014
PO 1650
9 8 7 6 5 4 3 2 1

Photo Credits:
Dreamstime: 24/25 Pancaketom, 8/9 Myroslav Prylypko, 10/11, 14/15
Olga Khoroshunova, 20/21 Luis Carlos Jiminez, 12/13 Nightbox, 16/17
Piccaya, 18/19 Roman Zaremba, 22/23 Ammit, Front cover, 28/29 Noam-
fein, 26/27 Propix; **Shutterstock:** 6/7 Dirk Ercken;

All dinosaur artworks courtesy of **IMP**

Contents

Introduction

Dinosaurs lived on Earth millions of years before we did. Even though no human being has ever seen a dinosaur, we still know a lot about them. Many dinosaur bones, teeth, or fossils have been found all over the world. Scientists have discovered what the dinosaurs looked like, how they moved, and what—or who—they ate. Dinosaur means "very terrible lizard."

Acrocanthosaurus

Acrocanthosaurus was one of the biggest meat-eaters of the Early Cretaceous period. It could even have tackled gigantic plant-eaters. Its huge, sharp teeth and long claws made it a swift and ruthless killer. Footprints discovered in the US show that it sped up to its prey and then lunged at its victim, slashing it to death with its teeth.

WHERE DID THEY LIVE?

Mainly in the southern states of Oklahoma and Texas, with some possibly east in Maryland.

US

Spines

Spines on the back may have been used for self-defense.

Claws

Vicious, hooked claws could rip at the flesh of prey and grip animals firmly.

FACTS

SIZE

- *Acrocanthosaurus* means "high spine."
- The jaws contained 68 thin, bladelike teeth.
- Lived during the Early Cretaceous period.

DID YOU KNOW?

 Acrocanthosaurus had a highly developed sense of smell. It would have been able to track its victims by scent.

The large eyes would have been able to spot prey at a distance. Above the eyes were hard "eyebrow bumps." These probably gave some protection from the claws of other killers.

The long, heavy tail balanced the animal's center of gravity over the hips. This kept it stable even when it was fighting.

Allosaurus

Allosaurus was a fearsome killing machine. It was fast, powerful, and able to attack anything it came across. It was the top predator for more than 10 million years. It seized prey with its muscular front limbs, inflicting terrible wounds with its sharp claws. It was a fast runner, but the top half of its body was heavy and it risked serious injury if it fell onto its short front arms.

WHERE DID THEY LIVE?

Mostly the US, with others found in Portugal, and possibly Tanzania and Australia.

Teeth

Each jaw had 30 or more teeth. New teeth grew to replace ones lost during fights.

Hands

Each hand had three sharp claws that could cut through flesh.

FACTS

SIZE

- *Allosaurus* means "strange lizard".

- The claws could be up to 6 in. (15 cm) long.

- Lived during the Late Jurassic period.

DID YOU KNOW?

This dinosaur's top half was very heavy. Without its massive tail to help with balance, it would have fallen over.

Allosaurus had a bony bump above each eye, and a bony ridge from the forehead to the tip of the snout. The purpose of this is not known, but it may have been a mark of rank among the dinosaurs.

The large muscular legs allowed it to sprint at prey. It may have emerged from trees close to water holes where it drank.

Archaeopteryx

Archaeopteryx is the earliest known bird. It had the teeth, claws, and tail of a killer dinosaur—and the feathers of a bird. It probably lived in open forests, gliding between trees. *Archaeopteryx* was about the size of a pigeon. Its mix of features suggests that it was a halfway stage in the development of birds from reptiles. Its remains hold clues to the evolution of flight in birds.

WHERE DID THEY LIVE?

Southern Germany. Limestone has preserved the impressions of its feathers.

Germany

Europe

Wings

The design of the wing was better suited for gliding than for flapping.

FACTS

SIZE

- *Archaeopteryx* means "ancient wing."

- Its feathers insulated the bird and controlled its body temperature.

- Lived during the Late Jurassic period.

Feet

Three toes pointed forward and one backward. This provided a good perching grip.

DID YOU KNOW?

 The jaws were lined with sharp, pointed teeth, like those of other meat-eating dinosaurs.

Debate continues about whether *Archaeopteryx* took off in flight by dropping out of trees or by running along the ground first in search of small animals to eat.

Modern birds have no tail bones, but *Archaeopteryx* had a long, bony tail more like a reptile.

Amargasaurus

One of the strangest dinosaurs ever discovered, *Amargasaurus* had a mane of bony spikes all the way down its neck and back. The double row of neck spikes would have made this dinosaur a hard target for hungry predators. Some experts think that the spikes on its back may have been covered with skin. This might have made an impressive display sail.

WHERE DID THEY LIVE?

The only remains are from the La Amarga canyon in Patagonia, west of Argentina.

South
America

Argentina

Spines

These long spines may have been strengthened by a horny covering.

FACTS

SIZE

- *Amargasaurus* means "lizard from La Amarga."

- The tallest neck spines were up to 20 in. (50 cm) long.

- Lived during the Early Cretaceous period.

Tail

Held out straight, the long tail would have counterbalanced the long neck.

DID YOU KNOW?

Amargasaurus had a small head. Its nostrils were right at the top of the skull, above its eyes.

This dinosaur was surprisingly light for its size. This was because its vertebrae (backbones) were partly hollow. This means it weighed less than if they had been made of solid bone.

The animal was probably not very agile because of its size. The long spines would have restricted the movement of its neck.

Gallimimus

Gallimimus was an Olympic sprinter of a dinosaur. Not many predators could have caught the birdlike beast as it sped along. It was half bird and half lizard, with a long, stiff tail, legs like an ostrich, and a toothless beak. It snapped up small creatures such as lizards, and perhaps even the buried eggs of other dinosaurs.

WHERE DID THEY LIVE?

Fossils have been found in the Bayshin Tsav region of southeastern Mongolia.

Mongolia

Asia

Hands

The hands ended in three long, flexible fingers tipped with small claws that could grip.

Eyes

Eyes on the side of its head suggest that *Gallimimus* would have had an all-around view.

FACTS

SIZE

- *Gallimimus* means "bird mimic."

- It was a fast runner and could possibly reach 43 mph (70 km/h).

- Lived during the Late Cretaceous period.

DID YOU KNOW?

Gallimimus walked upright on powerful back legs. If alarmed, the dinosaur could reach fast speeds over short distances.

Although it wasn't very well-known before, *Gallimimus* became famous in 1993 when a herd of them were featured in the movie *Jurassic Park*.

It may have eaten small insects, leaves, and berries, and possibly dinosaur eggs scooped from the ground with its claws or long, shovel-like bill.

Hypsilophodon

Not all plant-eating dinosaurs were big and slow. *Hypsilophodon* was so small and athletic that it could outrun most of its enemies. More than 20 skeletons were found close together on the Isle of Wight in the United Kingdom. This suggests that these animals lived in herds. It is not known how they died, but they may have been killed by a flood or drowned in quicksand.

WHERE DID THEY LIVE?

Fossils have been found on the Isle of Wight in the UK and in Portugal.

United Kingdom

Isle of Wight

Europe

Portugal

Eyes

Large eyes meant it would have seen well in the gloom of dusk and dawn.

Legs

Long shins and short, powerful thighs made *Hypsilophodon* a swift runner.

FACTS

- *Hypsilophodon* means "high-ridged tooth."

- A small, lightweight body allowed it to sprint away from trouble.

- Lived during the Early Cretaceous period.

SIZE

DID YOU KNOW?

Chisel-like teeth lined the back of its jaws. It was one of the few dinosaurs of its time to chew its food.

When *Hypsilophodon* was first discovered, experts mistakenly thought it was a young *Iguanodon*. It was only 20 years later that scientist Thomas Huxley realized it was a new dinosaur.

Five-fingered hands would have supported its weight when it leaned forward to feed from the ground.

Ouranosaurus

This big, heavy, plant-eating dinosaur had powerful jaws. They were perfect for tearing off and grinding up leaves. Fossil remains show that *Ouranosaurus* had extra-long spinal bones on its back. Some experts think that the bones supported a tall sail that the reptile used to maintain a comfortable temperature.

WHERE DID THEY LIVE?

Found in Niger, Africa, at a time when the region was almost as hot as it is today.

Niger

Africa

FACTS

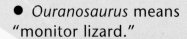

- *Ouranosaurus* means "monitor lizard."

- Its sail made it look bigger and may have scared away predators.

- Lived during the Early Cretaceous period.

SIZE

Spine

The long spine bones may have supported a "sail" to warm and cool the beast's blood.

DID YOU KNOW?

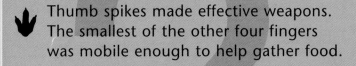 Thumb spikes made effective weapons. The smallest of the other four fingers was mobile enough to help gather food.

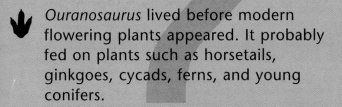 *Ouranosaurus* lived before modern flowering plants appeared. It probably fed on plants such as horsetails, ginkgoes, cycads, ferns, and young conifers.

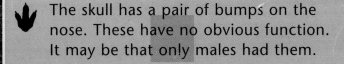 The skull has a pair of bumps on the nose. These have no obvious function. It may be that only males had them.

Tail

This helped balance if the animal reared up to feed on leaves high up in the trees.

Psittacosaurus

This scary-looking but harmless animal once lived in great numbers all over eastern Asia. *Psittacosaurus* had a sharp, parrotlike beak that it used to strip leaves off trees. It would only have been waist high against a human so it had long arms to pull down branches. It needed to eat a lot to get enough energy. It may have gathered in herds to fight against attackers.

WHERE DID THEY LIVE?

Found in Mongolia, Russia, China, and Thailand.

Russia ●
Mongolia
●
● China
●
Thailand

FACTS

● *Psittacosaurus* means "parrot lizard."

● There are more than 400 specimens of *Psittacosaurus*.

● Lived during the Early Cretaceous period.

SIZE

Beak

This was made from bone. At its tip was a rostral bone, a feature unique to horned dinosaurs.

DID YOU KNOW?

Some experts believe that *Psittacosaurus* relied on camouflage to hide from hungry killer dinosaurs.

The first *Psittacosaurus* fossil was found in 1922, on the American Museum of Natural History's third expedition to Mongolia. It was named the next year by US expert Henry Fairfield Osborn.

Arms

These were long enough to use to pass food to its mouth.

Some *Psittacosaurus* fossils contain smoothly polished pebbles. It swallowed stones to help with digestion.

Saltasaurus

Saltasaurus lived in South America about 75 million years ago. It was a member of a group of giant, long-necked dinosaurs called sauropods. They walked slowly, carefully, and quietly, like elephants. *Saltasaurus* had a long, sturdy tail that supported its weight as the leaf-eater reared up to feed on foliage high in the trees.

WHERE DID THEY LIVE?

Found in northwest Argentina in South America, in the area around Salta Province.

South
America

Argentina

Teeth

Peglike teeth stripped leaves off branches.

Armor

Well protected by its armor, which covered its back, tail, and neck.

FACTS

- *Saltasaurus* means "Salta lizard."
- *Saltasaurus* was an armored sauropod.
- Lived during the Late Cretaceous period.

SIZE

DID YOU KNOW?

Like many plant-eating dinosaurs, *Saltasaurus* had a very large body, a small head, and a long neck. This meant it could stretch up to reach leaves or fruit on high branches.

Saltasaurus was a very big dinosaur, but eggs of its close relatives found in 1997 in Patagonia, Argentina, were only around 4 in. (10 cm) long.

Some scientists believe that sauropods used their long tails as weapons, to inflict stinging blows on their enemies.

Suchomimus

Around 100 million years ago, a killer dinosaur terrorized the waters of Africa. *Suchomimus* probably waded into the water on its two legs and caught giant fish on the massive claws on its thumbs. It may also have hidden in the rushes, waiting for a dinosaur to bend down to drink. In a single lunge, its jaws could have crunched its victim's flesh and bones.

WHERE DID THEY LIVE?

The only known fossil was found in 1997, near the Tenere Desert of Niger, West Africa.

Niger

Africa

Spines

Tail spines along the backbone may have supported a fleshy fin.

FACTS

SIZE

- *Suchomimus* means "crocodile mimic."

- *Suchomimus* had about 100 teeth, which were not serrated.

- Lived during the Early Cretaceous period.

Teeth

These locked together, creating a narrow mesh from which fish could not escape.

DID YOU KNOW?

Nostrils sat on top of the snout like a crocodile's. This allowed the killer to lie hidden in the water.

The sail on its back may have been brightly colored for use in mating displays.

The sail may also have soaked up the sun's early-morning rays so that it warmed up quickly.

Triceratops

With a mighty, helmetlike head with horns, and weighing as much as a small automobile, *Triceratops* was a giant among dinosaurs. Few predators would have dared to pick a fight with it. On some adults, the eye-horns grew to more than 3 ft. (0.9 m) in length. *Triceratops* would have used these lethal weapons to fend off meat-eaters.

WHERE DID THEY LIVE?

Colorado, Wyoming, Montana, South Dakota in the US. Alberta and Saskatchewan, Canada.

North America

Teeth

Up to 40 columns
of teeth grew on
each side of its jaw.

FACTS

SIZE

- *Triceratops* means "three-horned face."

- Males possibly had larger skulls and horns than females.

- Lived during the Late Cretaceous period.

Horns

Three sharp horns
might have been
used to scare
off predators.

DID YOU KNOW?

 Most dinosaurs are known from just a few specimens, but the fossil finds of *Triceratops* include hundreds of skulls.

 With five teeth per column and 40 columns of each side of the jaw, *Triceratops* had 432 teeth in total. If any tooth was damaged or broken, another would grow in its place.

 Triceratops had pillarlike legs, a bit like those of a rhino, to support its huge, bulky body.

Tyrannosaurus

Tyrannosaurus was one of the largest and most terrifying creatures the world has known. It once lived in what is now North America. It was so strong that it would have been able to overpower almost any other animal around at the time. Its huge jaws were filled with daggerlike teeth that could rip prey apart with one or two bites.

WHERE DID THEY LIVE?

Found throughout western North America.

North America

Teeth

The huge teeth would have sliced skin and crunched bone easily.

FACTS

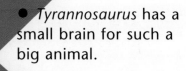

SIZE

- *Tyrannosaurus* means "tyrant lizard."
- *Tyrannosaurus* has a small brain for such a big animal.
- Lived during the Late Cretaceous period.

DID YOU KNOW?

- The skin of *Tyrannosaurus* was almost certainly covered in scales, like those on crocodiles.

- *Tyrannosaurus* young probably had feathers, but adult *Tyrannosaurus* didn't need feathers to control their body heat.

- *Tyrannosaurus* had bigger teeth than any other carnivorous dinosaur. The teeth in the upper jaw were larger than most of the teeth in the lower jaw. The largest was 13 in. (33 cm).

Arms

Experts disagree on the use of these two-fingered hands and tiny but powerful arms.

Glossary

armor – hard covering used to defend animals from attackers

carnivore – a meat-eating animal

Cretaceous – The period of geological time from 145 to 65 million years ago. It was the last of the three dinosaur periods.

fin – a winglike body part used to propel or balance an animal

flexible – something that can easily bend

fossils – prehistoric remains such as bones, or traces such as footprints, that have become preserved in rock.

horns – pointed bones that stick out from an animals' head. They can be used for attack or defense.

Jurassic – The period of geological time between 199 and 145 million years ago.

herd – a group of animals that live or travel together

lethal – deadly

muscular – having strong, powerful muscles

predator – animal that lives by killing other animals

prey – animals that are killed by other animals

reptile – a cold-blooded animal such as snakes, lizards, and dinosaurs

rostral bone – dinosaur bone on its upper jaw that forms a beak with the lower jaw

sauropods – dinosaurs that have a long neck and tail, small head, and 5-toed limbs

scales – a small, rigid plate that forms the outside covering of an animal

skeleton – the bones of an animal which form its protective structure or framework

snout – the large end of an animal's nose

sprint – to run very fast

Further Information:

Books

Dale, Jay. *Top 10 Dinosaurs.* Smart Apple Media, 2012.

Dixon, Dougal. *Dinosaurs Dominate: Jurassic Life.* New Forest Press, 2009.

Dixon, Dougal. *Meat-Eating Dinosaurs.* New Forest Press, 2011.

Miles, Liz. *Giant Dinosaurs.* Arcturus Publishing, 2012

O'Hearn, Michael. *Allosaurus vs. Brachiosaurus: Might Against Height.* Capstone Press, 2011.

Websites

http://science.nationalgeographic.com/science/prehistoric-world.html
Learn more about the prehistoric world

http://www2.lhric.org/pocantico/dinosaur/dinosaur.htm
Take a look at dinosaur reports and research by elementary school students

www.wmnh.com/wmbhi000.htm
View dinosaur fossils from the Black Hills Institute of Geological Research

http://www.enchantedlearning.com/subjects/dinosaurs/Dinotopics.html
A comprehensive look at dinosaurs for students of all ages

http://www.search4dinosaurs.com
A visual A-Z guide to all types of dinosaurs

Index: